MISSION TO MARS

MARS ORBITERS

BY
JOHN HAMILTON

Abdo & Daughters
An imprint of Abdo Publishing | abdopublishing.com

abdopublishing.com

Published by Abdo Publishing, a division of ABDO, PO Box 398166, Minneapolis, Minnesota 55439. Copyright © 2019 by Abdo Consulting Group, Inc. International copyrights reserved in all countries. No part of this book may be reproduced in any form without written permission from the publisher. Abdo & Daughters™ is a trademark and logo of Abdo Publishing.

Printed in the United States of America, North Mankato, Minnesota.
052018
092018

THIS BOOK CONTAINS
RECYCLED MATERIALS

Editor: Sue Hamilton
Copy Editor: Bridget O'Brien
Graphic Design: Sue Hamilton
Cover Design: Candice Keimig and Pakou Moua
Cover Photo: iStock
Interior Images: All Images NASA, except: European Space Agency-pgs 26, 27, 28, 29, 42 & 45 (Mars Express); Indian Space Research Organisation-pgs 36, 37 & 45 (Mars Orbiter Mission); iStock-pg 4; Shutterstock-pg 15; United Arab Emirates Space Agency-pg 43.

Library of Congress Control Number: 2017963900
Publisher's Cataloging-in-Publication Data
Names: Hamilton, John, author.
Title: Mars orbiters / by John Hamilton.
Description: Minneapolis, Minnesota : Abdo Publishing, 2019. | Series: Mission
     to Mars | Includes online resources and index.
Identifiers: ISBN 9781532115950 (lib.bdg.) | ISBN 9781532156885 (ebook)
Subjects: LCSH: Mars (Planet)--Orbit--Juvenile literature. | Mars (Planet)--
     Satellites--Juvenile literature. | Mars (Planet)--Ephemerides--Juvenile
     literature. | Mars (Planet)--Exploration--Juvenile literature.
Classification: DDC 523.43--dc23

CONTENTS

JOURNEY TO THE RED PLANET

For thousands of years, people have feared Mars, the Red Planet. They trembled at its rusty color and its strange wanderings through the night sky. Many wondered if an alien civilization lived on its surface, perhaps plotting an attack on an unsuspecting Earth. After all, in ancient Greek and Roman mythology, Mars was the god of war.

Mars, God of War

In more modern times, curious astronomers in the late 1800s gazed at Mars through Earth-bound telescopes. Mars appeared similar to Earth, even though its diameter is just 4,220 miles (6,791 km) at its equator. That is about half the size of our home planet. Even so, Mars is tilted on its axis, just like Earth. That gives the Red Planet seasons. There are polar ice caps, and bands of colors on the surface that seem to change from winter to summer. Could there possibly be life on Mars? Scientists were determined to find out.

A NASA illustration shows Mariner 4 headed for the mysterious planet of Mars.

In the early 1960s, the Soviet Union (most of which was today's Russia) launched a series of probes to explore Mars. All of them failed. In 1964, it was America's turn to try. That year, NASA's Mariner 4 space probe left Earth's orbit, bound for Mars. The discoveries it made changed our way of thinking about the Red Planet. In more recent years, a fleet of orbiters from several countries has followed Mariner 4, giving us new insight about mysterious Mars.

MARINER 4

Before sending orbiters to circle Mars, NASA scientists first had to prove they could send a spacecraft across the vast distances of space. Mariner 4's mission was to fly past Mars (a flyby) and take pictures to send back to Earth. The spacecraft was built tough to survive the harsh, cold conditions of deep space. It used four solar arrays to generate electricity.

Mariner 4 successfully launched at Cape Canaveral, Florida, on November 28, 1964. It rode atop a mighty Atlas-Agena rocket, bound for Mars. (The Mariner 3 Mars mission had failed earlier that month.) During the eight-month voyage, the spacecraft used the Sun and a bright star called Canopus to guide it through space. It traveled farther than any human-made object.

The Mariner 4 spacecraft was assembled by engineers and technicians at the Jet Propulsion Laboratory in Pasadena, California. Here it is prepared for a weight test on November 1, 1963.

MARINER 4			
Mission:	Mars flyby	Mars Arrival:	July 14, 1965
Launch:	November 28, 1964	Mission End:	December 21, 1967
Launch Vehicle:	Atlas-Agena D	Spacecraft weight (mass):	575 pounds (261 kg)

The first close-up image of Mars taken by Mariner 4.

On July 14, Mariner 4 flew about 6,118 miles (9,846 km) over the rusty colored surface of Mars. The probe's instruments came to life. Its primitive television camera (the best technology available) took 22 low-resolution pictures. They covered about one percent of the planet's surface. The images took a week to reach Earth because of slow computer speeds. The pictures revealed that Mars was a harsh wasteland. It was a dry, rocky planet filled with Moon-like craters. Mariner 4's other scientific instruments discovered that Mars has an atmosphere that is extremely thin. Liquid water would quickly evaporate in the Martian air. These facts shattered the hope that Mars was an inviting place that could harbor life. But the Red Planet still held many surprises, which scientists would soon discover.

MARINERS 6 AND 7

After the success of Mariner 4, NASA prepared more flyby missions. Mariner 5 went to Venus, but Mariners 6 and 7 were sent to Mars. They arrived at the Red Planet within four days of each other in the summer of 1969. Both spacecraft were modified versions of Mariner 4. They were bigger and heavier, and had improved scientific instruments on board. They carried fully automatic instrument packs that included two television cameras. They also carried infrared and ultraviolet spectrometers.

Mariner 7 is launched aboard an Atlas-Centaur rocket from Florida's Cape Canaveral on March 27, 1969.

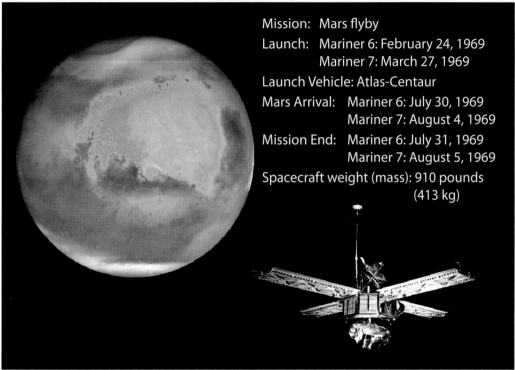

Mission: Mars flyby
Launch: Mariner 6: February 24, 1969
Mariner 7: March 27, 1969
Launch Vehicle: Atlas-Centaur
Mars Arrival: Mariner 6: July 30, 1969
Mariner 7: August 4, 1969
Mission End: Mariner 6: July 31, 1969
Mariner 7: August 5, 1969
Spacecraft weight (mass): 910 pounds
(413 kg)

Like Mariner 4, when Mariners 6 and 7 arrived at Mars, they took photographs and instrument readings. They then sped past the planet, slipping back into deep space. During their flyby missions, Mariners 6 and 7 took a combined 210 photos of Mars. The two probes increased the close-up coverage of Mars to nearly 10 percent of the Martian surface.

Mariners 6 and 7 confirmed much of what Mariner 4 already revealed. The desert-like surface of the planet was dotted with thousands of craters. Also, the Martian atmosphere was very thin, and there was no trace of a magnetic field like that on Earth. Mariner 7 recorded a surface temperature at the south pole of -190 degrees Fahrenheit (-123 degrees C). That made scientists believe that the Martian polar caps were made of sheets of frozen carbon dioxide.

MARINER 9

In 1969, Mariners 6 and 7 discovered exciting facts about Mars. They also raised more questions. To solve these new riddles, NASA scientists needed something more than a simple flyby mission. They needed a probe that could orbit the planet and investigate it for a long time. Two years later, they got their wish.

Mariner 9 was larger than the earlier Mariner probes, tipping the scales at 1,245 pounds (565 kg). Much of the extra weight came from a larger engine and extra fuel to help Mariner slow down once it reached Mars so it could enter orbit around the Red Planet.

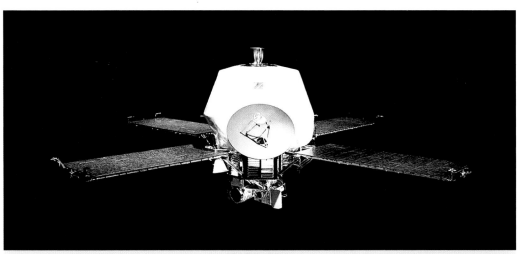

MARINER 9

Mission:	Mars orbiter	Mars Arrival:	November 14, 1971
Launch:	May 30, 1971	Mission End:	October 27, 1972
Launch Vehicle:	Atlas-Centaur	Spacecraft weight (mass):	2,200 pounds (998 kg)

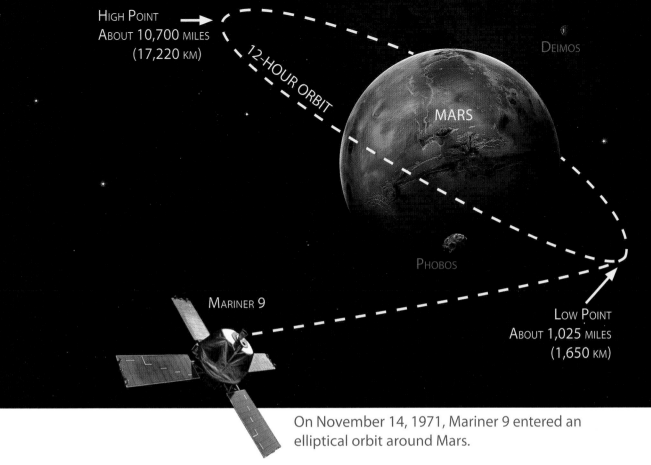

HIGH POINT →
ABOUT 10,700 MILES
(17,220 KM)

12-HOUR ORBIT

DEIMOS

MARS

PHOBOS

MARINER 9

LOW POINT
ABOUT 1,025 MILES
(1,650 KM)

On November 14, 1971, Mariner 9 entered an elliptical orbit around Mars.

Mariner 9 lifted off from Cape Canaveral on May 30, 1971. (Earlier that year, Mariner 8 failed 20 seconds after launch and crashed into the Atlantic Ocean.) Mariner 9's liftoff went smoothly, beginning a 247 million mile (398 million km) journey through deep space. Five months later, on November 14, 1971, Mariner 9 slipped into an elliptical orbit around Mars. It became the first spacecraft to orbit another planet. After two rocket burns to correct its orbit, it was ready to start its mission of examining Mars. At its closest approach, it was just 1,025 miles (1,650 km) above the Martian surface, much closer than any of the other Mariner probes.

Mariner 9's mission was delayed by a massive dust storm that covered much of the planet. Luckily, NASA could reprogram the spacecraft's computer. They shut off the probe's cameras to conserve energy while it waited out the storm.

After several weeks, Mariner 9's instruments were switched back on. The spacecraft began sending high-resolution photos back to Earth, along with other scientific measurements. For almost a full year, it returned 7,329 images of Mars. They covered nearly 85 percent of the planet's surface.

Scientists were astonished by the dramatic landscape they saw. A series of enormous shield volcanoes was discovered. The largest was Nix Olympica, which was later renamed Olympus Mons. It towers 16 miles (26 km) above the surrounding plains. The extinct volcano has a diameter of 374 miles (602 km). That is about the same area as the state of Arizona.

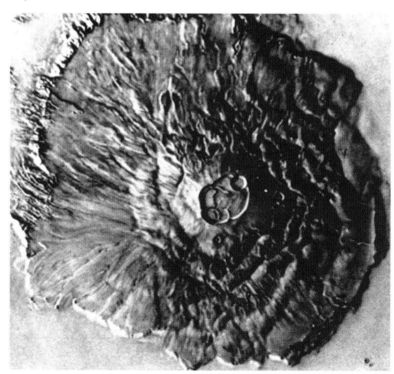

Mariner 9 captured a photo of an enormous shield volcano. Originally called Nix Olympica, it was later renamed Olympus Mons. The volcano is roughly the same area as the state of Arizona.

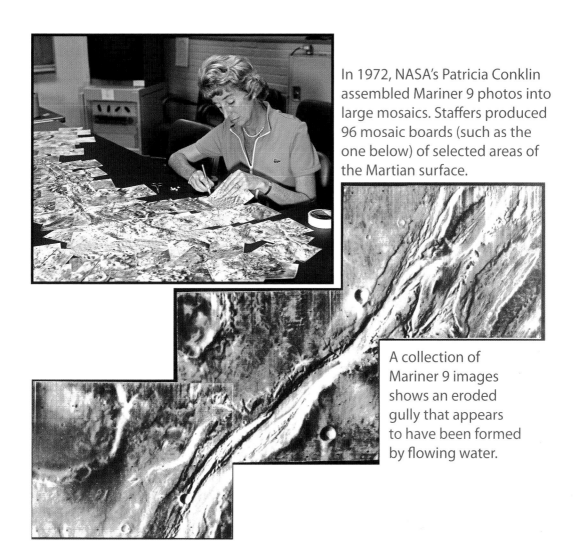

In 1972, NASA's Patricia Conklin assembled Mariner 9 photos into large mosaics. Staffers produced 96 mosaic boards (such as the one below) of selected areas of the Martian surface.

A collection of Mariner 9 images shows an eroded gully that appears to have been formed by flowing water.

Mariner 9 took photos of Valles Marineris, a massive canyon about 2,485 miles (4,000 km) long. The spacecraft also took the first close-up images of Mars's two moons, Phobos and Deimos.

Perhaps the most exciting images were those of ancient, dry riverbeds. Scientists were astonished. If water flowed on Mars long ago, it is possible there is still life clinging to the planet, maybe underground.

After a mission lasting nearly one year, Mariner 9 ran out of fuel and could no longer be controlled. The spacecraft was switched off on October 27, 1972. It remains in orbit around Mars today. It will probably crash into the planet sometime in the 2020s.

MARS 2 & 3

By 1971, the Soviet Union had launched many Mars-bound spacecraft. Several blew up immediately, or were lost shortly after launching. Some made it into space, but later lost contact with Earth. The Soviets used powerful rockets to lift heavy, complicated orbiters. Their spacecraft designs were ambitious, but they couldn't quite match the Americans in performance. Despite setbacks, the Space Race continued.

The Soviets launched a pair of spacecraft in May 1971. They were named Mars 2 and Mars 3. They were huge, each weighing more than 5 tons (4.5 metric tons). Unlike the American Mariner 9 spacecraft, they included landers to explore the surface of Mars.

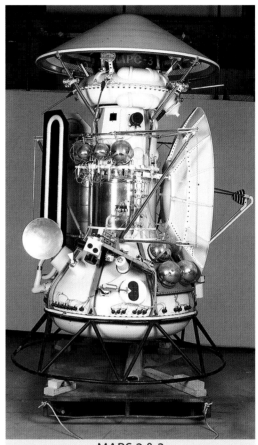

MARS 2 & 3

Mission: Mars orbiter/lander
Launch: Mars 2: May 19, 1971
Mars 3: May 28, 1971
Launch Vehicle: Proton K/Blok D
Mars Arrival: Mars 2: November 27, 1971
Mars 3: December 2, 1971
Mission End: August 22, 1972
Spacecraft
weight (mass): 10,250 pounds
(4,649 kg)

A 1973 stamp shows the journey of Mars 3. The Soviet spacecraft included an orbiter, lander, and even a small rover.

Mars 2 and Mars 3 arrived at the Red Planet a few days after Mariner 9. They encountered the same planet-wide dust storm that caused Mariner 9 to delay its mission. Unfortunately, the Soviet computers could not be reprogrammed from Earth. The probes circled the planet and dutifully took dozens of photos of the clouds swirling on the surface.

The Soviet landers also had bad luck. The Mars 2 lander crashed (becoming the first human object to reach Mars). The Mars 3 lander touched down safely with the help of parachutes and rockets. It sent a television image for a few seconds, and then contact was lost. Both Soviet missions, so close to becoming exciting breakthroughs, instead were disappointing failures.

VIKING 1 & 2

Viking 1 Liftoff

In 1972, the Mariner 9 orbiter sent back exciting high-resolution images of the surface of Mars. There were valleys and gullies that seemed to have been formed by erosion, probably from flowing water. Since water is one of the most important ingredients for life as we know it, could creatures have once existed on the Red Planet?

The cold, harsh conditions on the surface of Mars today make life nearly impossible. But could there be simple organisms thriving underground? That is a hard question to answer from high above. NASA was ready to take the next step: it would look for life by landing a spacecraft on the surface of Mars.

VIKING 1 & 2

Mission: Mars orbiter/lander

Launch: Viking 1: August 20, 1975
               Viking 2: September 9, 1975

Launch Vehicle: Titan III/Centaur

Mars Arrival: Viking 1: June 19, 1976
              Viking 2: August 7, 1976

Mission End:
   Viking 1 orbiter: August 17, 1980
   Viking 2 orbiter: July 25, 1978

Spacecraft weight (mass),
  orbiter only, with fuel: 5,125 pounds
                            (2,325 kg)

On August 20, 1975, Viking 1 blasted off from Florida's Cape Canaveral on a pillar of fire and smoke. After a 10-month journey through deep space, it arrived at Mars. It had a twin, Viking 2, which arrived a few weeks later.

Each spacecraft included two parts. A lander would conduct experiments on the Martian surface. An orbiter would take high-resolution color images while circling the planet. It would be the most complex mission ever to explore Mars.

The Viking 1 lander safely touched down on Mars on July 20, 1976. The Viking 2 lander followed on September 3, 1976. They took breathtaking photos and conducted many science experiments. They analyzed soil samples from just under the surface. They found many clues, but no firm evidence of life.

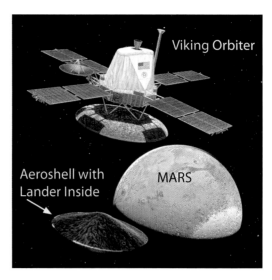

Meanwhile, high above the planet, the Viking orbiters carried out their missions. The orbiters were much bigger than the previous Mariner probes. Each weighed 5,125 pounds (2,325 kg). They were heavier because they carried more instruments and they needed more fuel to slow the spacecraft down when they reached Mars orbit.

The orbiters measured about 8 feet (2.4 m) across. They held scientific instruments, cameras, and antennas. Power came from 4 solar arrays. With the panels spread out, each orbiter measured about 32 feet (9.7 m) across. Mounted on the side of each spacecraft was the lander, nestled safely inside an "aeroshell." The landers piggybacked to Mars and then dropped to the Martian surface.

The Viking orbiters captured images of Mars's two moons, Phobos and Deimos, in 1977.

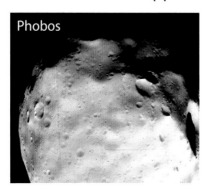

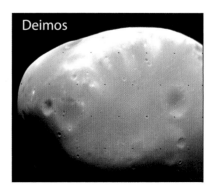

More than 100 images, taken by the Viking 1 orbiter, were combined to create this image of Mars. In the middle of the planet is the Valles Marineris canyon, about 2,485 miles (4,000 km) long and 6 miles (10 km) deep.

Even though the landers were the stars of the mission, the two Viking orbiters had very important jobs. Their high-resolution color cameras helped scientists choose the safest landing sites possible for the landers. They eventually mapped most of the planet's surface, sending about 52,000 color photographs to Earth by radio. They also took detailed photos of Mars's two moons, Phobos and Deimos. The orbiters also discovered that permafrost, frozen water, lies just beneath the Martian surface. In addition, the ice cap at the north pole contains vast amounts of frozen water.

The Viking orbiters lasted much longer than expected. After several years and hundreds of orbits, each spacecraft was eventually powered down by NASA. The Viking missions were a huge success, but much was yet to be learned about Mars.

MARS GLOBAL SURVEYOR

I n August 1993, NASA lost its Mars Observer spacecraft. It was designed to study the Red Planet's climate, magnetic field, and atmosphere. It was also equipped to take high-resolution photos of the surface. Unfortunately, the probe suffered a fatal fuel leak. All contact was lost just three days before it was due to orbit Mars.

NASA replaced the doomed Mars Observer with a new, lower-cost orbiter called Mars Global Surveyor. On September 12, 1997, it arrived at Mars. Once it reached the planet, it used a new way to slow down called aerobraking. It went into a long, looping orbit. When it was closest to Mars, the spacecraft dipped slightly into the atmosphere. This caused a force called drag to slow the orbiter slightly. After repeated orbits lasting over a year, Mars Global Surveyor settled into a circular orbit just 280 miles (451 km) above the Martian surface.

MARS GLOBAL SURVEYOR

Mission: Mars orbiter
Launch: Nov. 7, 1996
Launch Vehicle: Delta II
Mars Arrival: Sept. 12, 1997

Mission End: Nov. 2, 2006
Spacecraft weight (mass): 2,272 pounds (1,031 kg)

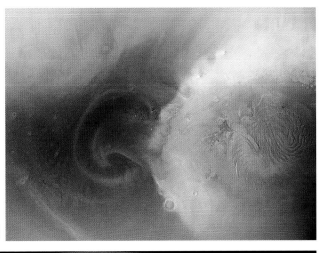

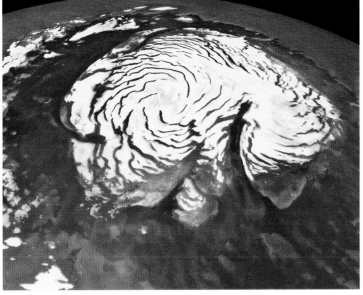

Mars Global Surveyor took images of Mars for more than nine years. These are some of the amazing photos, including the Galle Crater or "Happy Face Crater," a dust storm on the planet, and a view of Mars's north pole covered in ice.

Mars Global Surveyor was a big success. For more than nine years, the sturdy orbiter took thousands of high-quality images of Mars and its two moons. Using the probe's data and images, scientists learned about the role of water in Mars's past, and how it carved parts of the landscape. And it studied Mars's atmosphere and weather patterns. It even captured a real-time image of a dust devil and the tracks left behind in the soil.

2001 MARS ODYSSEY

In 1999, NASA lost its Mars Climate Orbiter spacecraft. It was designed to study Mars's atmosphere and climate. That same year, the space agency also lost the Mars Polar Lander, which crashed on the surface. Losing two Mars spacecraft in one year was a disaster. Losing the Mars Climate Orbiter was especially embarrassing. NASA used metric system measurements (kilometers, meters, etc.). Unfortunately, the company that built the spacecraft and supplied its software used American units (miles, feet, etc.). The difference in measurement caused the spacecraft to aerobrake too deeply into Mars's atmosphere, where it broke up during its first orbit.

Planetary scientists have a saying that "Mars is hard." Of the many spacecraft that have been sent to the Red Planet, about half have been lost or destroyed for various reasons. Was there a space monster that lurked near Mars, feasting on spacecraft? One NASA engineer joked that it was the Great Galactic Ghoul.

A NASA illustration of the Great Galactic Ghoul with an orbiter.

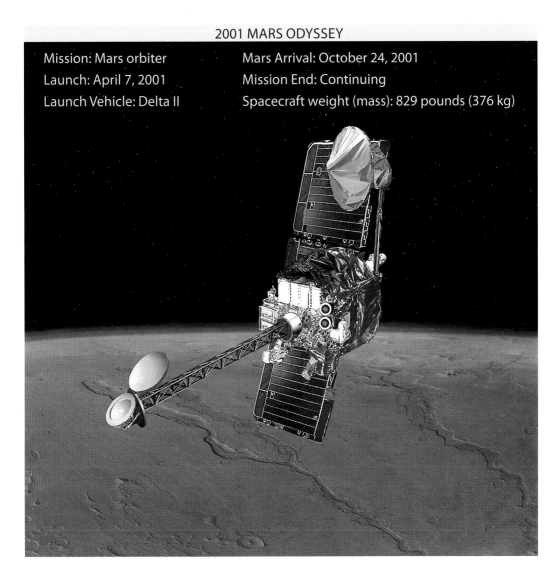

Mission: Mars orbiter

Launch: April 7, 2001

Launch Vehicle: Delta II

Mars Arrival: October 24, 2001

Mission End: Continuing

Spacecraft weight (mass): 829 pounds (376 kg)

In 2001, NASA tried again. On April 7, 2001, the 2001 Mars Odyssey spacecraft blasted off from Florida's Cape Canaveral. The probe was named to honor science fiction author Arthur C. Clarke and his masterpiece, *2001: A Space Odyssey*. After a six-month journey through the void of space, it arrived safely at Mars. As with the earlier Mars Global Surveyor spacecraft, Odyssey used aerobraking to slow down and settle into an orbit around the planet.

The 2001 Mars Odyssey orbiter is shaped like a large box. For power, it uses a three-panel solar array that sticks out of one side. Also projecting from the spacecraft is an antenna, a gamma ray spectrometer, a thermal camera, plus other instruments. They measure the amounts of water, ice, and minerals in the Martian soil.

The spacecraft had a device that measured radiation harmful to astronauts on the planet's surface. (The equipment broke down in 2003, but most of its mission was completed.) Odyssey also acts as a radio relay for Mars rovers that explore the surface.

Odyssey spent years and hundreds of orbits mapping and analyzing Mars. It discovered massive amounts of water ice under the Martian soil. Early in the planet's history, Mars was covered with oceans and rivers. Scientists have always wondered what happened to all the water. Odyssey seems to have solved that mystery: much of the water seeped deep into the soil and froze into underground glaciers and polar ice sheets.

The 2001 Mars Odyssey spacecraft continues exploring the Red Planet and acting as a radio relay for surface rovers. As of 2018, it is the longest-serving Mars orbiter. If it stays healthy, it could continue operating at least until the mid-2020s.

This view of Noctis Labyrinthus is a combination of images taken by 2001 Mars Odyssey from April 2003 to September 2005. Odyssey is the longest-working Mars orbiter in history.

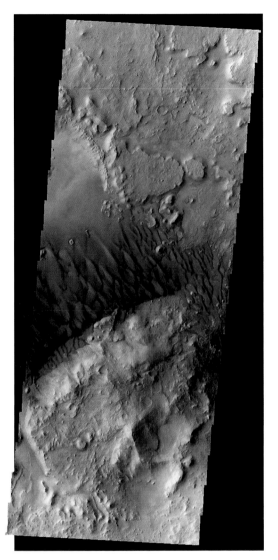

Mars Odyssey's THEMIS VIS camera took this false color image of the dune field in the Arabia Terra crater. Sand appears as a blue to dark blue color. The smaller areas of sand are easily visible and indicate the large amount of available material for creating dunes. The shape of the dunes show that prevailing winds have come from different directions over the years.

Fans and ribbons of dark sand dunes creep across the floor of Mars's Bunge Crater in response to winds blowing from the direction at the top of the picture. Mars Odyssey's Thermal Emission Imaging System took this image in 2010. The complete image shows an area of the Red Planet that is about 9 miles (14 km) wide.

MARS EXPRESS

O n December 25, 2003, another orbiter arrived at Mars, but it wasn't from NASA. The European Space Agency (ESA) today plays a major role in space exploration. It has been building and flying spacecraft and equipment since the late 1970s. Its members represent 22 European countries, including France, the United Kingdom, Germany, and Italy.

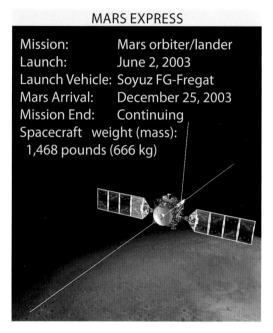

MARS EXPRESS

Mission:	Mars orbiter/lander
Launch:	June 2, 2003
Launch Vehicle:	Soyuz FG-Fregat
Mars Arrival:	December 25, 2003
Mission End:	Continuing
Spacecraft weight (mass):	1,468 pounds (666 kg)

The Mars Express orbiter is ESA's first try at visiting another planet. So far it has been very successful. As of 2018, it continues orbiting Mars and sending back data to Earth. It is the second-longest working probe circling Mars (behind NASA's 2001 Mars Odyssey spacecraft).

The main goal of Mars Express is to explore the geology and atmosphere of Mars. The probe has a high-resolution stereo camera, as well as sensitive spectrometers and radar. It can detect water and ice as deep as 3 miles (5 km) below the Martian surface.

Mars Express blasted off on June 2, 2003, from the Russian Baikonur Cosmodrome inside the Republic of Kazakhstan. It used Russian-built Soyuz FG-Fregat rockets. It was named Mars Express because of how fast and efficiently it was built. Also, its voyage was fast because Earth and Mars were very close together when the spacecraft was launched.

A photo of Candor Chasma taken by the High-Resolution Stereo Camera (HRSC) on Mars Express.

Several days before Mars Express entered Martian orbit, it released Beagle 2, a lander that was meant to search for signs of life on the surface. Unfortunately, its solar panels did not unfold properly after landing and Beagle 2 could not communicate with Earth.

The Mars Express orbiter, on the other hand, performed its job with flying colors. It was the first probe to detect water ice at the Martian south pole, hidden underneath thick sheets of frozen carbon dioxide (dry ice). It also detected traces of methane in the atmosphere. The methane may have come from volcanic activity, or it may have been evidence of some sort of life form, perhaps microbes in the soil. Future spacecraft will investigate further.

Mars Express continues to map the Martian surface and search for water trapped underground. Its cameras have sent home stunning views of the Red Planet. With its large reserves of fuel, the spacecraft should continue operating into the 2020s or beyond.

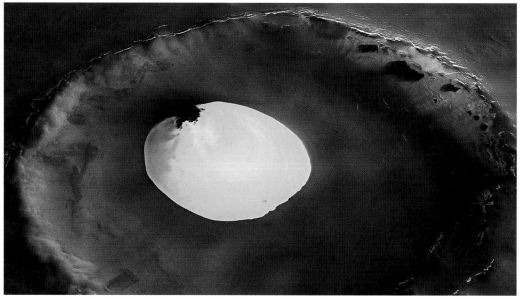

Water ice is photographed by Mars Express at the bottom of a crater near the Martian north pole.

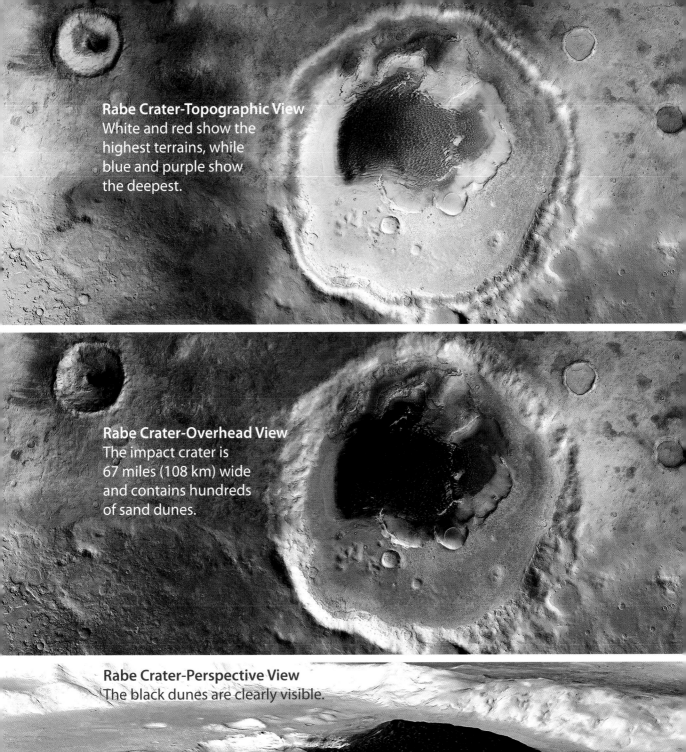

Rabe Crater-Topographic View
White and red show the highest terrains, while blue and purple show the deepest.

Rabe Crater-Overhead View
The impact crater is 67 miles (108 km) wide and contains hundreds of sand dunes.

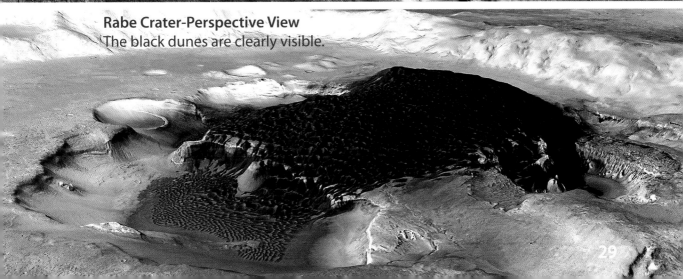

Rabe Crater-Perspective View
The black dunes are clearly visible.

MARS RECONNAISSANCE ORBITER

I n 2005, NASA readied its next spacecraft to explore the Red Planet. The Mars Reconnaissance Orbiter (MRO) had similar instruments as previous spacecraft, including Mars Global Surveyor and 2001 Mars Odyssey. However, MRO was equipped with greatly improved technology. Its spectrometers and

MARS RECONNAISSANCE ORBITER

Mission: Mars orbiter	Mission End: Continuing
Launch: August 12, 2005	Spacecraft weight (mass):
Launch Vehicle: Atlas V	2,273 pounds (1,031 kg)
Mars Arrival: March 10, 2006	

radar are able to give the best readings yet of the kinds of minerals found on Mars, and how much water ice is buried beneath the surface.

MRO is equipped with a telescope camera called the High Resolution Imaging Science Experiment (HiRISE). It is much larger and more powerful than any camera previously sent to Mars. It can make out objects as small as 3 feet (.9 m) across, or about the length of a guitar. (Previous orbiters could pick out surface details about the size of a school bus.)

Mars Reconnaissance Orbiter High Gain Antenna (HGA) is installed in June 2005. In orbit around Mars, it sends vast amounts of data back to Earth.

MRO has a huge radio dish antenna. It measures about 10 feet (3 m) across. It was designed to handle the vast amounts of data the orbiter sends back to Earth from its high-resolution camera and scientific instruments. The large antenna and computer capacity are also used to relay many radio signals from other spacecraft, including rovers on the Martian surface.

Mars Reconnaissance Orbiter blasted off from Florida's Cape Canaveral on August 12, 2005. By March 2006, it arrived safely at Mars. After 6 months of aerobraking, it settled into a circular orbit about 175 miles (282 km) above the planet.

MRO's high-resolution camera was used to pinpoint safe sites for Mars landers. It can detect medium-sized boulders that might cause a lander to crash. In 2008, NASA's Phoenix Lander spacecraft had its landing site changed after MRO detected too many boulders in the original target. (Phoenix landed safely on May 25, 2008.)

MRO began its journey to Mars on August 12, 2005.

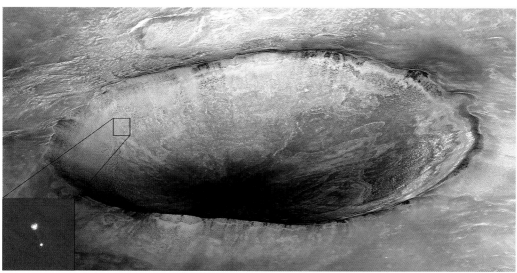

Mars Reconnaissance Orbiter helps find safe sites for Mars landers. This MRO image shows the Phoenix lander and its parachute as it drops to the Red Planet in 2008.

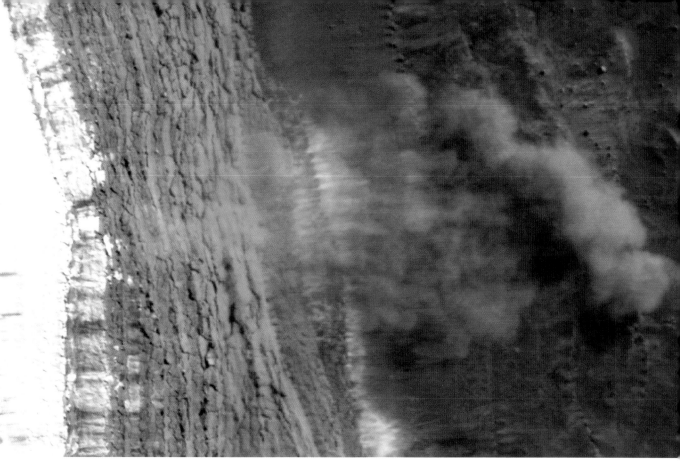

An avalanche on the Red Planet is captured by the Mars Reconnaissance Orbiter.

After several years of collecting science data and images, MRO discovered many new things about Mars. It took photos of brand-new craters made by meteorites. Some of the craters showed water ice scattered in the ground thrown up by the impact. The water ice rapidly evaporated because of the thin Martian atmosphere. The probe took close-up photos of Mars's two moons, Phobos and Deimos. MRO also took photos of dust devils swirling on the surface of Mars, and found evidence of fresh avalanches in craters and canyons.

By 2015, MRO had sent back to Earth more data than all the previous missions to Mars combined. It equaled more than 14 billion pages of printed data. It continues its mission today, and will probably operate until the 2020s or later.

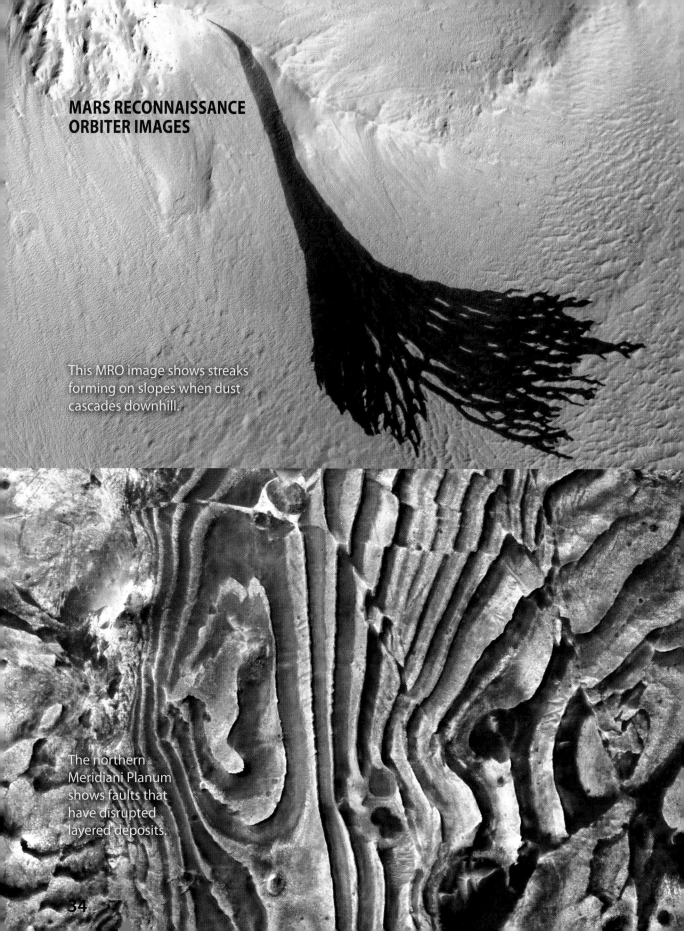

MARS RECONNAISSANCE ORBITER IMAGES

This MRO image shows streaks forming on slopes when dust cascades downhill.

The northern Meridiani Planum shows faults that have disrupted layered deposits.

34

This image was originally meant to track
the movement of sand dunes near the
north pole of Mars, but the piles of boulders
on the ground in between the dunes also
interested scientists.

In spring, the ice on the smooth surface of some Mars dunes cracks. The escaping gas
carries dark sand out from the dune below, often creating beautiful patterns.

MANGALYAAN

The Mangalyaan spacecraft is a Mars orbiter from India. Also called the Mars Orbiter Mission, it is the country's first interplanetary probe. India's space agency is called the Indian Space Research Organisation (ISRO). It is only the fourth space agency to reach Mars, behind NASA, the European Space Agency, and the Soviet Union's space program. It was the first Asian spacecraft to reach Mars.

Mangalyaan (a Sanskrit name that means "Mars craft") followed India's successful Moon orbiter mission in 2008. The Mars mission was planned as a demonstration of technology. The scientists at ISRO wanted to prove they could achieve such a goal at a very low cost. Remarkably, they succeeded on their very first try.

MANGALYAAN

Mission: Mars orbiter
Launch: November 5, 2013
Launch Vehicle: Polar Satellite
Mars Arrival: September 24, 2014
Mission End: Continuing
Spacecraft weight (mass):
  2,948 pounds (1,337 kg)

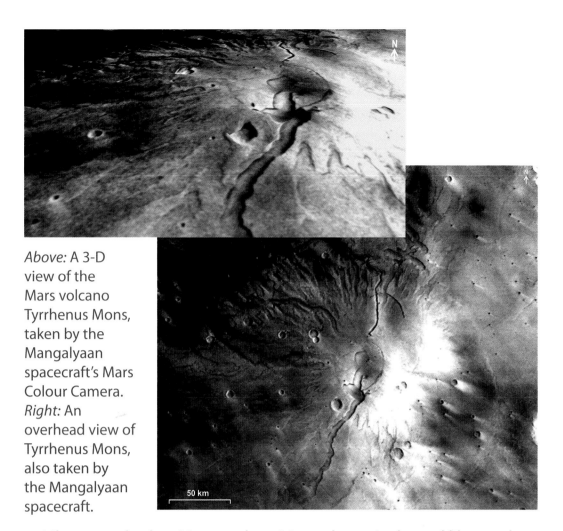

Above: A 3-D view of the Mars volcano Tyrrhenus Mons, taken by the Mangalyaan spacecraft's Mars Colour Camera. *Right:* An overhead view of Tyrrhenus Mons, also taken by the Mangalyaan spacecraft.

50 km

Like several other Mars probes, Mangalyaan is shaped like a cube. It has solar arrays projecting from one side. It also has a large antenna and several scientific instruments. They include a spectrometer, a methane sensor, and a high-resolution camera.

Mangalyaan blasted off from India's Satish Dhawan Space Centre on November 5, 2013. It entered Mars orbit on September 24, 2014. It then began exploring features on the Martian surface, as well as investigating the planet's atmosphere. It tracked the amount of dust in the Martian sky, and measured the surface temperature of the planet. It also took rare close-up photos of the backside view of Deimos, one of Mars's two moons. Now that its main mission is complete, Mangalyaan has enough fuel to continue exploring Mars for many years.

MAVEN

hy did Mars dry out? That is the big question that NASA's MAVEN Mars orbiter was sent to investigate. MAVEN stands for Mars Atmosphere and Volatile Evolution. The spacecraft was designed to study the Martian atmosphere and to find out why so much of it vanished into space.

MAVEN has no camera. Instead, it contains instruments that measure the solar wind and how it erodes Mars's atmosphere. It also has a magnetometer to precisely measure the planet's weak magnetic field.

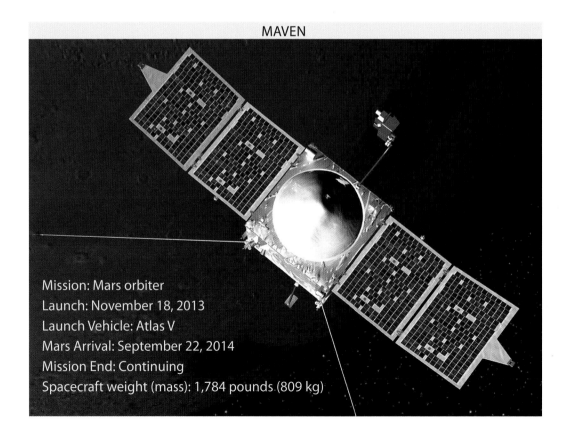

MAVEN

Mission: Mars orbiter
Launch: November 18, 2013
Launch Vehicle: Atlas V
Mars Arrival: September 22, 2014
Mission End: Continuing
Spacecraft weight (mass): 1,784 pounds (809 kg)

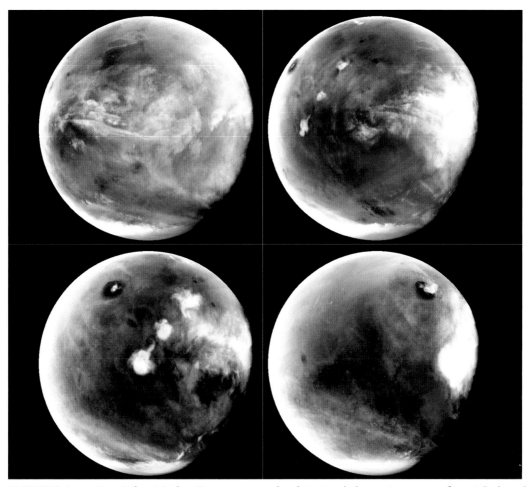

MAVEN's Imaging UltraViolet Spectrograph obtained these images of rapid cloud formation on Mars. White clouds over Mars's volcanoes are easily seen.

Without a strong magnetic field (like Earth's), charged particles from the Sun (the solar wind) can cause a planet's atmosphere to slowly be stripped away. Early in its history, Mars had oceans of water and a much thicker atmosphere. But without a protective magnetic field, the solar wind over billions of years reduced Mars's atmosphere by almost 99 percent. Today, the atmosphere is so thin that liquid water cannot exist on the surface because it almost instantly evaporates.

During its main mission, MAVEN shed light on this process. It also proved that atmospheric erosion greatly increases in intensity during solar storms. The orbiter will likely continue collecting data into the 2020s.

FUTURE MISSIONS

InSight is a NASA robotic lander. It will use underground probes to learn about the deep interior of Mars. It successfully launched on May 5, 2018, from California's Vandenberg Air Force Base. If all goes well, InSight should arrive at Mars in November 2018.

An engineer tests the solar arrays on one of the Mars Cube One (MarCO) spacecraft at NASA's Jet Propulsion Laboratory. Two of these mini-satellites will travel with the InSight lander on its mission to Mars in 2018. They are designed to relay data about InSight's entry, descent, and landing back to Earth.

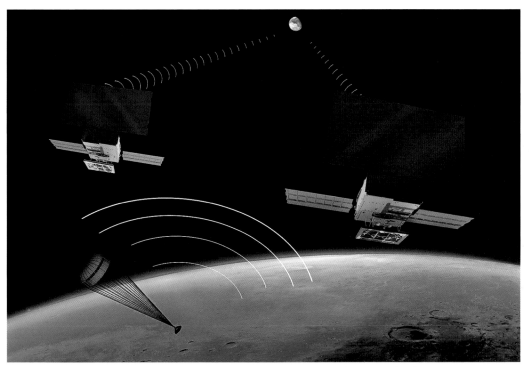

Two CubeSats are scheduled to fly past Mars just as the InSight lander descends to the planet's surface. The CubeSats will provide an experimental communications relay to inform Earth quickly about the landing.

Tagging along with InSight are two briefcase-sized spacecraft called CubeSats. They are part of a mission called Mars Cube One (MarCO). The twin CubeSats are equipped with radio antennas and solar panels for power. When the InSight lander descends to the surface, the CubeSats will relay information to scientists on Earth in just minutes. Otherwise, communications might be delayed for hours until other orbiters get in the proper position to relay data.

If the MarCO mission is successful, these small satellites could be used by future landers and rovers as inexpensive relays for communicating with Earth. They can also be customized to perform other missions. They can help explore not only Mars, but also other planets and objects in our solar system.

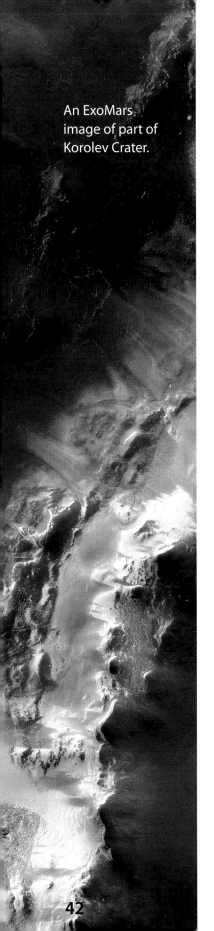

An ExoMars image of part of Korolev Crater.

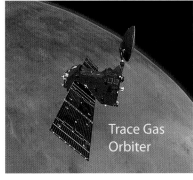

Trace Gas Orbiter

ExoMars is a joint mission of the European Space Agency (ESA) and Roscosmos, the Russian space agency. ExoMars consists of four spacecraft on two different rockets launched separately. The first part was launched on March 14, 2016. It reached Mars in October 2016. A lander called Schiaparelli crashed on the surface, but the Trace Gas Orbiter is successfully circling the planet. (The second part of ExoMars, which includes a rover, will launch sometime in 2020.)

The ExoMars Trace Gas Orbiter spacecraft is looking for small amounts of methane in the Martian atmosphere. Methane is produced by geological activity, such as volcanos. It is also given off by some living creatures, such as microbes. The orbiter will also hunt for other chemicals. If it finds methane combined with propane or ethane, that would be a strong signal that microbes exist on Mars, perhaps under the surface. If the orbiter detects methane with sulfur dioxide, then the methane probably comes from volcanic activity. Results from the orbiter's experiments are due sometime in 2018 or 2019.

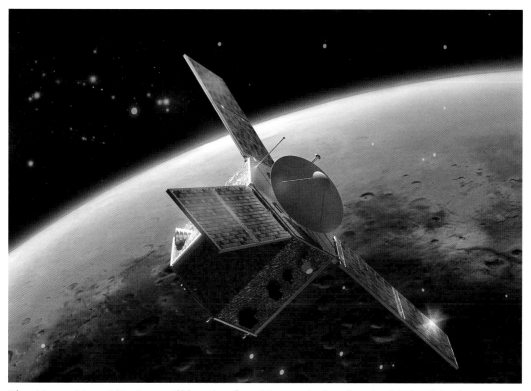

The Hope Mars Mission will be the first Mars mission by the United Arab Emirates (UAE) Space Agency. The probe is due to launch in 2020.

The Hope Mars Mission probe is due to launch in the summer of 2020. About the size of a small car, it is being designed and built by scientists from the United Arab Emirates. It will be the first Mars mission launched by any Arab or Muslim nation. If it arrives safely at Mars, it will explore the planet's atmosphere and climate.

More countries than ever before are planning missions to Mars. Spacecraft technology continues to improve, and hard lessons are learned from past mistakes. New spacecraft sent to Mars build upon the successes—and failures—of the missions that went before them. Our knowledge grows with each journey to the mysterious Red Planet.

TIMELINE

Mariner 4

July 14, 1965—Mariner 4 (USA) flyby. The spacecraft takes 22 low-resolution photos of Mars, revealing a dry, rocky planet filled with Moon-like craters.

July 30, 1969—Mariner 6 (USA) flyby. Comes within 2,136 miles (3,437 km) of Martian equatorial surface.

Mariner 6 & 7

Aug. 4, 1969—Mariner 7 (USA) flyby. Records temperature at south pole of -190° Fahrenheit (-123° C).

Nov. 14, 1971—Mariner 9 (USA) arrives at Mars. First spacecraft to orbit another planet.

Mariner 9

Nov. 27, 1971—The Soviet Union's Mars 2 orbiter arrives at Mars. Lander crashes, becoming first human object to reach surface of planet.

Dec. 2, 1971—Mars 3 orbiter arrives at Mars. Along with Mars 2, automatically takes photos of featureless dust storm raging on planet. Mars 3 lander touches down on surface but malfunctions after a few seconds.

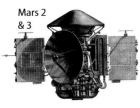
Mars 2 & 3

June 19, 1976—Viking 1 (USA) orbiter arrives at Mars. On July 20, accompanying Viking lander is first spacecraft to safely land on surface and complete its mission of photographing Martian landscape and analyzing soil.

Viking 1 & 2

Aug. 7, 1976—Viking 2 (USA) orbiter arrives at Mars. Lander safely touches down on surface. The two Viking orbiters send nearly 52,000 color images of the Martian surface to Earth.

Sept. 12, 1997—Mars Global Surveyor (USA) arrives in orbit around Mars using aerobraking to slow its speed. Takes thousands of photos of Mars and its two moons.

Oct. 24, 2001—2001 Mars Odyssey (USA) enters Mars orbit. Discovers massive amounts of water ice under the Martian surface. It is the longest-serving Mars orbiter to date.

Dec. 25, 2003—The European Space Agency's Mars Express orbiter arrives at Mars. Explores geology and atmosphere of the planet, takes high-resolution stereo images. Accompanying Beagle 2 lander fails.

March 10, 2006—Mars Reconnaissance Orbiter (USA) begins orbiting Mars. Telescope camera takes high-resolution images of planet's surface. Other instruments explore different minerals on Mars, and water ice trapped under surface. Acts as radio relay for other spacecraft on surface or in orbit around Mars.

Sept. 24, 2014—Mangalyaan (Mars Orbital Mission) arrives at Mars. First Mars mission from India. Explores the Martian atmosphere and surface details.

Sept. 22, 2014—MAVEN (USA) orbiter enters orbit around Mars. Investigates how Martian atmosphere is affected by the solar wind.

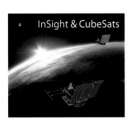

May 5, 2018—InSight (USA) lander blasts off from Vandenberg Air Force Base, California. If successful, it will land in November 2018. Two small CubeSat spacecraft accompany it. They will monitor landing and relay communications to Earth.

GLOSSARY

European Space Agency (ESA)

A space agency, like NASA, that builds and flies spacecraft that explore the solar system. Its headquarters is in Paris, France. As of 2018, there are 22 countries that are members of the ESA.

Flyby

When a spacecraft travels close to a planet or other object but does not enter into an orbit around it. During a flyby, a spacecraft has one chance to take as many photos and gather as much scientific data as possible before it sails off to its next destination.

National Aeronautics and Space Administration (NASA)

A United States government space agency started in 1958. NASA's goals include space exploration, as well as increasing people's understanding of Earth, our solar system, and the universe.

Orbit

The circular path a moon or spacecraft makes when traveling around a planet or other large celestial body. There are several satellites orbiting Mars, including NASA's Mars Reconnaissance Orbiter and the European Space Agency's ExoMars Trace Gas Orbiter.

Probe

An unmanned space vehicle that is sent on missions that are too dangerous, or would take too long, for human astronauts to accomplish. Probes are equipped with many scientific instruments, like cameras and radiation detectors. Information from these instruments is radioed back to ground controllers on Earth.

Rover

A robotic vehicle that is driven over rough terrain by remote control.

SOLAR WIND

Streams of charged particles that are given off by stars. Solar wind is a plasma of electrons, protons, and other particles. They are so energetic they can escape from the Sun's gravity.

SOVIET UNION

A former country that included a union of Russia and several other communist republics. It was formed in 1922 and existed until 1991.

SPACE RACE

The Space Race was a competition between the United States and the former Soviet Union (much of which is today's Russia). It started in the mid-1950s and lasted until the early 1970s. By the mid-1960s, both countries had sent probes to Venus. Mars was the next prize.

SPECTROMETER

A spectrometer is a recording device that lets scientists collect data about light (the electromagnetic spectrum) that humans can't see, such as gamma rays, x-rays, microwaves, and radio waves. Light that humans can see is called "visible light." It is just a small part of the entire electromagnetic spectrum.

TELESCOPE

A device to detect and observe distant objects by their reflection or emission of various kinds of electromagnetic radiation (like light).

ONLINE RESOURCES

Booklinks
NONFICTION NETWORK
FREE! ONLINE NONFICTION RESOURCES

To learn more about Mars orbiters, visit abdobooklinks.com. These links are routinely monitored and updated to provide the most current information available.

INDEX